IT'S YOUR MOVE

ON BOARD

TWELVE INTERACTIVE GAME-BASED
SMALL GROUP SESSIONS

TOM ELLSWORTH

Standard®
PUBLISHING

Cincinnati, Ohio

Published by Standard Publishing, Cincinnati, Ohio

www.standardpub.com

Copyright © 2010 by Tom Ellsworth

Printed in: USA

Cover design: DesignWorks

Interior design: Dorcas Design & Typesetting

ISBN 978-0-7847-2363-0

15 14 13 12 11 10   1 2 3 4 5 6 7 8 9

CONTENTS

HOW TO PLAY THIS BOOK

The It's Your Move small group series was designed to get your group playing, interacting, talking, and connecting together through the study of God's Word and will for your lives. Here are some gaming tips on how to get the most out of this experience.

Each topic is divided into two parts: **GAME ON** and **POSTGAME BREAKDOWN**. These sessions were conceived as happening in two separate, consecutive small group meetings. However, you may of course choose to use them in whatever way works best for your group.

In **GAME ON**, group members play a board game together and talk briefly about the themes presented in that particular game. The six games used throughout the book are classics that have been around for some time, thus it is likely that the members of your group or other people you know will have a copy (or copies) that you will be able to borrow for use in your small group meeting. Depending on how much time and how many players you have available, you may choose to play one entire game, hold a tournament, or use one of the abbreviated versions of the game that has been suggested. If your group has members with children who also attend the small group meetings, it's easy to include them in the fun. We have offered suggestions for how to do that for each game session.

Further discussion on the game's themes and what the Bible has to say about these issues is carried on in the second session—**POSTGAME BREAKDOWN**. You will be given a Bible passage to study along with questions and commentary that help you dig deep into the meaning of God's Word. As you work through these studies, be sure to allow each person to have a chance to take part in making connections—this part is not a competition! Allow everyone an opportunity to voice their opinions.

Throughout the book, you will notice two kinds of questions, which we've titled **Take Turns** and **Your Spin**. The **Take Turns** questions are meant for group conversation, while the **Your Spin** questions are intended for personal exploration, though you may choose to share those answers with your fellow members as you wish. At the end of each of the postgame sessions you will find practical ideas for your group to take action and make your move by reaching out to your world in tangible ways. This could even develop into a third session for your group, a time when you meet to work and serve others together.

We hope you and your group enjoy these twelve interactive sessions. There's a lot here for you to experience as you build your relationships with God and each other. What are you waiting for? It's your move.

MONOPOLY:

Obsessing Over Things That Don't Last

PART ONE—GAME ON

Object of the Game

The MONOPOLY game triggers our competitive nature more quickly than many board games. Since winning is determined by the amount of one's property and cash reserves, greed often becomes the driving force. As you play this MONOPOLY round, use the game as a barometer of your own greed and insatiable desire for more.

Game Preparation

For this session you will need at least one edition of the MONOPOLY game, paper and pencil for each player and, of course, snacks. Buying property and building hotels makes a person hungry.

> "There is no dignity quite so impressive, and no independence quite so important, as living within your means
>
> —Calvin Coolidge, 30th U.S. President

Depending on the size of your small group, you may choose to use more than one game board so that every person is able to play. Or you can choose to play with teams around a single board. If you use one board, draw straws to determine teams. Avoid having husbands and wives on the same team; players may learn more about their spouses by watching how they make decisions as opponents.

Before any player throws the dice and moves past Go, take a moment to discuss a couple of questions:

- You may not have lived through the Great Depression of the 1930s, but perhaps you know someone who did. How did people cope with the difficulties of the time?

- Periodically our country's economy suffers dips and plunges. How do these low periods impact your finances? your family? your faith?

As you play the game, jot down a few notes about your reactions. Note any undesirable attitudes in yourself or others around the board. Review your notes later after the heat of competition has cooled. What did you learn about yourself and others in your small group?

TRIVIA

In 1930 the devastation of the Great Depression had settled over Germantown, Pennsylvania, like a thick, hopeless fog. Charles Darrow was broke and out of work, with no promise of relief in sight. In an effort to take his mind off his misery, Charles sat down at his kitchen table and sketched out some streets on a piece of oilcloth. The street names hailed from Atlantic City, a favorite vacation spot for him and his wife back in their prosperous days. Baltic Avenue. Park Place. Boardwalk. To this desirable real estate he added four railroads and a utility company. From scrap molding he cut out tiny houses and hotels. He gathered up bits and pieces of cardboard and typed out Deed cards for the properties. Free paint sample cards were used to decorate the game board, and colored buttons became tokens. Darrow rounded up as much play money as he could find and "The Game," as he called it, was complete.

Darrow and his wife played the game nightly and for a brief moment felt rich even in their poverty. Soon friends and neighbors wanted their own sets. The Darrows renamed it MONOPOLY, started making sets by hand, and sold them for $4 each. Eventually, Charles couldn't keep up with the demand and enlisted a local printer to help him make printed sets. These sold well enough to attract the interest of Parker Brothers, who had previously turned down similar versions of the game, including what is thought to be the original form of the game, patented in 1904 by Elizabeth Magie as the Landlord's Game. However, with Darrow's added flair for design and some other improvements, his game was selling so well, Parker Brothers couldn't ignore the popularity. They struck a deal, and in a true rags-to-riches story, Charles Darrow became the first millionaire from the profits of a board game.

Playing by the Rules

Here is a reminder to every player: the competitive spirit varies from one person to the next. Make sure all group members are included in the game regardless how aggressive or passive their participation.

Given the lengthy nature of the game, you may not have time to play a full version. Try this abbreviated version (play is the same with the following exceptions):

- Once the game-specified money has been distributed, shuffle the property cards and randomly deal them out to all players until all cards have been distributed.

- Each player begins with three houses, which can only be used after three properties of the same color are acquired.

- Property cards can be traded at the beginning of each player's turn before rolling the dice.

- Set a time limit on the game—the person with the most accumulated value at the end of the time period is declared the winner.

Want to spice up the game? Have each player or team roll the dice—the two top-scoring players or teams receive twice as much money as what is specified in the game rules while the others receive only half as much. How does this inequity change the mood of the game?

Too volatile? Here's a more equitable approach. Before the outset of the game, establish different criteria for winning. Try this idea. Give each player three minutes to write down his or her goals for the game: a certain amount of money, property, houses, etc. Set a time limit on the game play. The winner is the person who comes closest to reaching the goal when the time is up.

To Eat

Here are a few ideas for simple snacks to fit the theme:

- Chocolate coins, PayDay Bars, or 100 Grand Bars—have these candy treats scattered around to set a rich mood.

- "Bringing home the dough" sandwiches—your favorite meat and/or cheese on whole wheat bread cut in a rectangular shape about the size of a dollar bill.

- Silver dollar pancakes—(pancakes the size of silver dollars) kids will love them!
- Three Coins Carrot Salad—a healthy choice where the carrot slices look like copper coins. The simple recipe is as follows:

M I X I T U P

2 POUNDS CARROTS, SLICED IN CIRCLE SHAPES, COOKED, AND DRAINED	1 TEASPOON PREPARED MUSTARD
	1 TEASPOON SALT
	1 TEASPOON PEPPER
1 CAN TOMATO SOUP	2 GREEN PEPPERS, SEEDED AND SLICED IN STRIPS
¾ CUP VINEGAR	
½ CUP OIL	2 LARGE ONIONS, CHOPPED
1 CUP SUGAR	

Mix soup, vinegar, oil, sugar, mustard, salt, and pepper. Mix carrots, peppers, and onions. Pour liquid mixture over vegetables and marinate overnight.

For Younger Players

If they are old enough to play a MONOPOLY game on their own, you could engage children who also attend your group meetings in one of the newer, kid-friendly versions such as the Chronicles of Narnia or Disney MONOPOLY games. If age-appropriate, try the newer version that uses MONOPOLY credit cards instead of money. There are over one hundred versions of the game to choose from, so at least one is bound to please.

If you don't have enough kids to play a game, or if they are too young, employ them in the adult game as bankers, realtors, or contractors. They will feel included as they dole out the cash, shuffle through the properties, and hand out the houses and hotels. Look for ways to teach important lessons on spending, greedy attitudes, the danger of debt, etc. as the game progresses.

Picking Up the Pieces

After the winning tycoon has been declared, take a few minutes to close with prayer. Begin by reading Matthew 6:25-34. Do your financial concerns create a sense of inflated anxiety? Are your priorities as confusing as the tax code? Ask God to increase:

- your financial wisdom.

- your conviction to seek first his kingdom and his righteousness.

- your trust in his ability to provide for your needs.

TAKE TURNS

1. Did you find anything surprising or interesting about the way people played this game? If you played as teams, what did you learn about your partners?

2. What was your attitude toward your money? Did you count it often? Did you try to protect your stash?

3. How did you treat the other players? How did you feel about those who owed you rent? How did you react if they couldn't pay?

MONOPOLY:
Obsessing Over Things That Don't Last

PART TWO—POSTGAME BREAKDOWN

Object of the Study

You've had some time to think about your insights learned in playing the MONOPOLY game as a group; now let's contemplate what Jesus said about our desire for possessions.

Bible Content

Today's concerns associated with money and materialism are nothing new. Jesus confronted these regularly in his earthly ministry. Luke records one such incident and the subsequent parable that Jesus used to confront the problem.

> Someone in the crowd said to him, "Teacher, tell my brother to divide the inheritance with me."
>
> Jesus replied, "Man, who appointed me a judge or an arbiter between you?" Then he said to them, "Watch out! Be on your guard against all kinds of greed; a man's life does not consist in the abundance of his possessions."
>
> And he told them this parable: "The ground of a certain rich man produced a good crop. He thought to himself, 'What shall I do? I have no place to store my crops.'
>
> "Then he said, 'This is what I'll do. I will tear down my barns and build bigger ones, and there I will store all my grain and my goods. And I'll say to myself, "You have plenty of good things laid up for many years. Take life easy; eat, drink and be merry."'
>
> "But God said to him, 'You fool! This very night your life will be demanded from you. Then who will get what you have prepared for yourself?'
>
> "This is how it will be with anyone who stores up things for himself but is not rich toward God."
>
> —Luke 12:13-21

To Study

Did you notice how the conversation began? Here is a man who has the ear of the Master Teacher . . . God in the flesh. What an opportunity to be able to ask God anything you want! What would you have asked?

- Teacher, how can I make my life pleasing to you?

- Teacher, what is Heaven like?

- Teacher, can you ever forgive me?

But our first-century counterpart doesn't inquire, he demands. "Teacher, tell my brother to divide the inheritance with me."

Why are we so blinded by financial issues? Money and possessions have separated more families than nearly any other conflict. Siblings easily become estranged over an inheritance. I once even heard of a man who cleaned out the house while the rest of his siblings were still at the funeral.

Money is also a major source of stress in marriages. The late Larry Burkett, a Christian financial expert, wrote that 95 percent of the couples he counseled were in financial trouble due to overspending by the husband. He noted that women tend to splurge on things like clothes and food. Men tend to splurge on things like new cars, boats, and airplanes. I wonder what the man in Luke's Gospel wanted to buy.

TAKE TURNS

1. How many times in the last month have you asked God a question about money, either directly or indirectly?

2. How many times in the last month have you asked God for help with your relationships?

3. What motivates you to ask God for help with these issues?

Given the fact that riches, material things, and financial security dominate so much of what we do, it should come as no surprise that these also dominated the lives of first-century people. Human nature has changed little over time.

YOUR ⟋ SPIN

1. A friend asks you for money advice. What do you do?

2. A relative asks to borrow money. What do you do?

3. Finances become the source of arguments between you and your loved one. When the subject comes up next, what do you do?

MATERIALISM MONOPOLIZES PRIORITIES

"Then he said to them, 'Watch out! Be on your guard against all kinds of greed; a man's life does not consist in the abundance of his possessions.'" The key word is greed. Jesus didn't say "guard against material things" or "guard against a savings or retirement account" or "guard against being rich." He said, "Guard against all kinds of greed." The problem is not in the amount but in the attitude. It's not how much one has but how what he has makes him behave.

Greed is a powerful, insatiable desire for more. I get a little crazy when I spot a classic car. My delirium and finger-pointing used to startle my family; now they just roll their eyes and ignore me. I have made the comment often, "If I could afford them, I would have a barn full of antique cars." There is a touch of greed in me, and when I see a beautifully restored 1940 Packard, I get a bad case of the "wants." I suspect there is a touch of greed in you also. What's your greed-trigger?

Take a look again at Mr. Monopoly, the main character in Jesus' parable. What was his problem?

MONOPOLY

- Fact: he was rich. Resources are from God and are to be used to serve him. Wealth was not the problem.

- Fact: he was successful. Using God-given abilities to make the most of life's opportunities honors the Lord. Success was not his problem.

- Fact: he was ambitious. Laziness, not ambition, is condemned in Scripture: "If a man is lazy, the rafters sag; if his hands are idle, the house leaks" (Ecclesiastes 10:18). Ambition was not his problem.

- Fact: he was goal oriented. Have you ever read about the apostle Paul? This great preacher set goals throughout his ministry, many of which God honored. Being goal oriented was not the farmer's problem.

- Fact: he was confused about his priorities. His greed for goods was greater than his need for God. *That* was the heart of his problem.

Most of us also struggle with the same imbalance of priorities. The Federal Reserve offered this recent information on debt (as found at http://www.money-zine.com/Financial-Planning/Debt-Consolidation/Credit-Card-Debt-Statistics, consulted 2/24/09):

- Americans charged approximately $2,052 billion to their credit cards in 2005—that's just over $12,500 in charges each year per cardholder.

- The average household in 2008 carried nearly $8,700 in credit card debt.

- As of the twelve months ending June 2006, there were 1.5 million consumer bankruptcy filings.

TAKE TURNS

1. Do you know someone who struggles with greed? What are the obvious signs?

2. What are some ways people could begin tomorrow to reduce indebtedness?

3. Share with each other your greed-triggers. Can you recognize your own? What types of things could people visualize or think about as greed-antidotes?

Balance is a spiritual issue. When the desire for more things outweighs the desire for more of God, our priorities are skewed.

YOUR SPIN

Regarding your priorities, see if the following statements are true or false.

1. _____ I have purchased things I didn't really need and couldn't afford.

2. _____ I have failed to buy necessities so I could buy what I wanted.

3. _____ I spend more than I earn.

4. _____ I have used my offering money to buy something for me.

MATERIALISM MONOPOLIZES FOCUS

Barns were a symbol of wealth in the first century—the bigger the barn, the wealthier the man. In other words, our farmer not only wanted to be rich, he wanted to look rich.

For the sake of his image and material security, the man hoarded more grain than he could use. Hoarded grain doesn't last very long—when stored too long, good grain sours and rots. Instead of giving to others, the farmer chose to keep it for himself even at the risk of spoilage.

Hoarding is the antithesis of living by faith. A hoarder loses focus and no longer has a need to trust God. Trust becomes *self-focused*.

Did you know that according to the Federal Reserve Board, the growth of consumers' unpaid debt on credit cards and other revolving accounts has escalated each year to its present price tag of over $2 trillion?

The farmer in the parable isn't the only one who's built bigger barns to store his stuff. According to the Self Storage Association (www.selfstorage.org), rentable self-storage capacity increased by 633 percent from 1985–2008, making storage units the fastest-growing sector of the commercial real estate market. With over 52,750 facilities scattered across the land, storage capacity now equals 7.24 square feet per person in America!

We know all of this stuff we have will not satisfy, right? Solomon wrote in Ecclesiastes 2:18, 19, "I hated all the things I had toiled for under the sun, because I must leave them to the one who comes after me. And who knows whether he will be a wise man or a fool? Yet he will have control over all the work into which I have poured my effort and skill under the sun. This too is meaningless."

Yet still we hurry around the squares, buying up everything we land on. Playing the MONOPOLY game may very well demonstrate how things hinder our relationships, confuse our priorities, and obscure our spiritual vision. But in the end, all that stuff goes back in the box.

Jesus concludes his parable with the impending death of the farmer and this warning: "This is how it will be with anyone who stores up things for himself but is not rich toward God." When our focus is God, we end up with a lot more than could fit in any box. When our focus is God, everything else falls into its proper place.

TAKE • TURNS

Go around the group and tell about your own experiences of "building bigger barns."

1. Give an example of modern-day hoarding that you've witnessed. Did the hoarding represent an emotional problem or a spiritual one? Explain.

2. What are you saving and storing that you don't need or won't use?

3. How does holding on to our material possessions keep us from growing closer to God?

It's Your Move!

Take a stroll through your closets and wardrobes. Dig deep in your dressers and chests. Box up all the forgotten items and the clothes that mysteriously shrank, and give them away.

As a group, deliver the gently used items to a mission that specializes in recycling used clothes for those who are in need. Perhaps your group can spearhead a clothing drive for the congregation or even engage your whole community as participants.

Check out local benevolence agencies. Perhaps you can coordinate a special clothing collection for those agencies, volunteer your time to help work at their sites, or devise a plan to raise community awareness regarding the local need.

Master Provisions is an organization that distributes much-needed clothing around the globe through clothing outlets that also provide jobs for out-of-work Christians. Learn more at: www.masterprovisions.org.

Don't have a local agency that fills this need? Perhaps your congregation could start one. Brainstorm together as a group to do what will work the best for your community.

Success in God's eyes isn't about what you have, but who you serve. So move right on past Park Place and Boardwalk. Be faithful to the Lord, and you'll someday walk on streets of gold!

LIFE:

PART ONE—GAME ON

Object of the Game

No game can adequately prepare a person for real life. Playing THE GAME OF LIFE board game can, however, give you some insight into the choices ahead of you. Pay close attention to your passions, possessions, and purposes as you twist and turn around the board. Think about how you respond to the positives and negatives of everyday living as revealed in your play.

Game Preparation

Each game can accommodate up to six players, so provide enough game boards for each member of your small group to have a seat at a table. You can also play as teams, in which case you might get by with only one game board. Since the game comes with pink and blue stick people for your game-piece vehicle, you might decorate with some pink and blue balloons, or even toy cars. And since the game highlights major moments

> "You only live once. But if you work it right, once is enough."
> —Fred Allen, comedian

TAKE 🎲 TURNS

After you shuffle the LIFE tiles and distribute the appropriate amount of funny money, try this exercise:

1. Point to the place on the game board that best represents the stage of your current life. Think and/or talk about how long it took you to reach that stage.

2. Ask each other these questions: What has been your greatest life challenge thus far? What is the best life lesson you have learned?

in life, you could put up a few streamers and banners, such as: Happy Birthday, Congratulations Graduate, Just Married (with a few dangling tin cans), Welcome to Your New Home, and Happy Retirement. The decorations provide a festive atmosphere that turns a mere game into more of an experience.

Want to practice up for the big game night? There is a free downloadable PC version available at: http://www.download-free-games.com/board_game_down load/game_of_life.htm. With great graphics and computer animation, it's another exciting way to experience THE GAME OF LIFE board game.

TRIVIA

Struggling for years to find success, Milton finally stumbled onto what he thought was a sure thing. The Republican National Convention suggested that he produce photos of their newly nominated presidential candidate. Scraping together enough money to purchase a lithograph press, he went to work printing thousands of pictures. The Republican candidate of 1860 did indeed win, but by the time Abraham Lincoln was headed for the White House, he had grown a beard and no one wanted Milton's photos of a clean-shaven Abe.

With thousands of unsold pictures and the nation on the brink of Civil War, his business seemed doomed. But just when all appeared lost, a game creator came along and breathed new life into Milton's enterprise. Milton printed up 45,000 copies of The Checkered Game of Life, and they sold like hotcakes. Eight years later Milton Bradley's company had become the nation's largest producer of games. To celebrate its centennial in 1960, the company launched a new game created by inventor Reuben Klamer and inspired by the original 1860s version. THE GAME OF LIFE board game has since become an American favorite.

Playing by the Rules

This game is fairly straightforward—be the player with the most material goods when the game is over, and you win. Playing by Milton Bradley's rules is OK, but I would suggest a little change that can make a big difference: if your group is made up of couples, have them play together as teams. If you have six couples or fewer in your small group, all could play around one game board. It will make the table area crowded, but when the Career, Salary, House Deeds, and Stocks cards come into play, the interaction between married or dating partners will be worth it. Who knows? An intense game might provide a reality check for some couples in your group. It might also spark some good follow-up conversations.

Here's another option. Instead of allowing each player to choose the college or career path at the beginning, draw straws to determine who must go to college and who must start a career. Now you have only two teams—the Greeks (those living it up in the fraternity or sorority) and the Grunts (those working stiffs with their noses to the grindstone). Play continues individually, but you play for a team victory. Each individual's accumulated wealth is added to the overall team score at the end of the game. Team members can share advice with one another as their collaborative efforts may help their team advance. Be strategic. One player may make a personal sacrifice if it advances the team's chance of winning. Caution: this version is not for the faint of heart. Competition can get fierce!

When the first player or team reaches Millionaire Estates, that's when the questions should begin:

- What was your worst decision in the game? Your best decision? How did these decisions impact you at the end of the game?
- Have you faced similar decisions or choices in real life? What's one of the best decisions you've ever made, and how has it made a genuine difference in your daily living?

To Eat

- Provide a variety of sweet breads (banana bread, zucchini bread, pumpkin bread, etc.) and label the tray "The Staff of Life."
- Try this Southwestern Snack Mix made with Life cereal. (You might also use Life cereal boxes to help decorate your tables.)

MIX IT UP

8 CUPS QUAKER® OAT LIFE CEREAL	2 TEASPOONS DRY CORIANDER
3 TABLESPOONS VEGETABLE OIL	2 TEASPOONS GARLIC POWDER
3 TABLESPOONS DRY TACO SEASONING MIX	1 CUP SALT-FREE OR REGULAR PRETZEL STICKS
2 TEASPOONS CRUSHED RED PEPPERS	1 CUP CORN CHIPS

Put cereal in a large bowl. Add vegetable oil and mix to coat cereal. Pour cereal into a 2-gallon storage bag. Combine taco seasoning and spices, then add to the bag. Close the bag securely and shake the mixture gently until cereal is well coated. Add pretzels and corn chips to the bag and toss again. Store in the bag or in an airtight container. For more information on Quaker recipes, go to www.quakeroats.com/cooking-and-recipes.aspx.

For Younger Players

There are kid-friendly versions of this game available to appeal to a variety of age groups. There's even an updated, modern version of the game called THE GAME OF LIFE TWISTS & TURNS. If you have kids who are old enough to play on their own, you could let them use one of these versions. Or you can involve kids in your game. Talk with them about how to make the most of the "life" you've been given in the game. Let them make some of your decisions. You could also make the following positions available for them to play:

- Dr. Bambino, Chief of Staff at the hospital's maternity ward—releases the pink and blue babies to live with their new families.
- Ima Teller, bank employee—keeper of the money.
- Sharky, CEO of the venerable Savings and Loan—takes care of loans and insurance.
- Dr. C. N. Future, career counselor—handles the Career, Salary, House Deeds, and Stocks cards.

Picking Up the Pieces

Life is God's gift to us; how we live it is our gift to God. Every day brings new challenges that test the mettle of our character. Living life as a solo act is not a smart move, especially since the creator of all life has willingly made his wisdom available to us. Jesus said, "I have come that they may have life, and have it to the full" (John 10:10). How has following Jesus made your life more "full"?

Read Philippians 1:21-24 in unison. What does Paul mean when he writes, "For to me, to live is Christ and to die is gain"?

Close your time together by sharing together and praying about the following issues. Ask God to help you prepare for:

- something you need to die to and something you need to live for.

- a life challenge, big or small, that you currently face.

- a spiritual victory you desire in your life.

LIFE:
Cherishing God's Gift

PART TWO—POSTGAME BREAKDOWN

Object of the Study

What's the goal of your life? This game ends just like the proclamation I once saw on a rusty old Ford's bumper sticker: "Whoever dies with the most toys wins!" But what does God want for us? Let's find out what we should do with his precious gift to us.

Bible Content

Paul's mission travels took him to the European continent where he was the first to preach the gospel in Greece. While in Athens, this is the message he shared with the Epicurean and Stoic philosophers.

> "The God who made the world and everything in it is the
> Lord of heaven and earth and does not live in temples built by
> hands. And he is not served by human hands, as if he needed
> anything, because he himself gives all men life and breath
> and everything else. From one man he made every nation
> of men, that they should inhabit the whole earth; and he
> determined the times set for them and the exact places where
> they should live. God did this so that men would seek him and
> perhaps reach out for him and find him, though he is not far
> from each one of us. 'For in him we live and move and have our
> being.' As some of your own poets have said, 'We are his off-
> spring.'
>
> "Therefore since we are God's offspring, we should not think
> that the divine being is like gold or silver or stone—an image
> made by man's design and skill. In the past God overlooked
> such ignorance, but now he commands all people everywhere
> to repent. For he has set a day when he will judge the world
> with justice by the man he has appointed. He has given proof of
> this to all men by raising him from the dead."
>
> —Acts 17:24-31

To Study

We are not much different from the people in ancient Athens. The answers the sought are answers we long to know. In his address, Paul provides an insightfu answer to an intriguing, universal question: Why did God give us life?

WAS IT TO *BUILD* SOMETHING FOR HIM?

During a teaching visit to TCM International in Austria, we toured some cathedral that literally took my breath away. These ornately styled and exquisitely detaile buildings are dedicated to the worship of God. As I entered their ancient door: I felt anything louder than a whisper would dishonor what seemed so sacred. doubt that such workmanship could even be duplicated today. Decades of labo and the sacrifice of thousands were required to construct these cathedrals as tribute to the worship of God.

And while God may well be honored by the people who built and worshipped i those hallowed places, he did not *need* those buildings. He cannot be contained i structures of wood and stone. He cannot be strapped to an altar as if that is wher we meet him. He cannot be confined to the height and breadth of any structure. A beautiful as these monolithic cathedrals are, they cannot compare to the cathedra of God's universe. From the starry heavens to the depths of the sea, no huma design can compare to the simplest of his creation. God didn't give us life becaus he needed us to build anything for him.

TAKE TURNS

1. Throughout history people have been captivated with the idea of building things for God—altars, monuments, cathedrals, and more. Why? What motivates people to build something for God?

2. Have you ever been in a man-made place that felt sacred? What made it feel that way to you? Was it because of what was made or because of who it was made for?

3. What kinds of things do you do because you believe God is expecting you to do something for him?

YOUR SPIN

Think about it. Are you more comfortable with . . .

1. A God who has a to-do list for you or who wants a relationship with you?

2. Doing acts of service or praying for a servant's heart?

3. Making a plan or following a plan?

AS IT TO *DO* SOMETHING FOR HIM?

ne of our daughters is a speech pathologist, the other a nurse. I remind them egularly how grateful I am to have two skilled professionals who can take care of 1e in my old age. God, however, doesn't need us to do something for him as if he helpless, injured, sick, or weak. He did not give us life so we could take care of im in his old age. God is not frail! He is all sufficient, and self-sufficient. If all of us sappeared in the next minute, he would not be diminished in the least. God does ot need us to *do* anything for him.

AS IT TO *PLAN* SOMETHING FOR HIM?

id you notice what Paul said to the Athenians? "From one man he made every ation of men, that they should inhabit the whole earth; and he determined the mes set for them and the exact places where they should live." Sounds like a plan me. What a disaster the universe would have been if God had consulted with human committee before creation! How many times in human history has God tervened to save us from ourselves? It is God who has guided history—the rise id fall of nations, the times and the seasons, the beginning and end. God doesn't eed us to *plan* anything for him.

TAKE TURNS

1. Do you have a plan for your life, or do you just go with the flow?

2. What do you think is the most important goal of your life?

3. What have you done to try to reach that goal?

4. What have you done to try to reach God's goals for your life?

So why DID he do it?

The answer is found in Paul's address: "God did this so that men would seek him and perhaps reach out for him and find him, though he is not far from each one of us." Did you catch it? He gave us life so we could have a relationship with him. Christianity isn't a religion; it's a relationship.

As Paul walked the streets of Athens, he was "greatly distressed to see that the city was full of idols" (Acts 17:16). He spoke with people in the synagogue and marketplaces, telling them the good news of Jesus. His teaching on the resurrection created such a stir among the Athenians that they brought him before the Areopagus, their leading judicial and philosophical council. Paul addressed these leaders: "Men of Athens! I see that in every way you are very religious. For as I walked around and looked carefully at your objects of worship, I even found an altar with this inscription: TO AN UNKNOWN GOD. Now what you worship as something unknown I am going to proclaim to you."

IT'S YOUR MOVE—ON BOARD

Paul did not criticize their ignorance nor id he respond angrily to their idolatry. He 1et them where they were spiritually 1d tried to lead them to the one true od. The Athenians were religious Jt not relational in their faith. How 1any people have you known like 1at? They seek the truth, but do ot test for it. Or maybe they never et past the religious ritual to dis- over the relational God. Or maybe 1ey find God, but then live their lives as they don't know who he is.

An 1860 version of this game became the inspiration for our modern-day THE GAME OF LIFE board game. However, the conclusions of the two games differed. In the original, the winner was not the one who finished with the most stuff, but the one who made proper moral decisions throughout the game and retired in peace. Now that's a great formula for victory!

God doesn't need us but he does want us. He created us first and foremost to be :lational. We were not created as slaves to do his bidding, or as toys to entertain m, or as puppets to be controlled by him. God created us as free-willed people so e would choose him. Paul said as much to those in the coliseum. God is not far vay—he is waiting for us, hoping we'll search for him and reach out to him. And hen we do honestly seek him, you can be sure we'll find him because he urgently ants to be found!

TAKE 🎲 TURNS

1. Why do you think many people embrace the idea of being spiritual, but reject the opportunity to know the Holy Spirit?

2. Have you ever experienced a time when you were looking for God, but found something else? What made you realize you had not found what you were looking for?

3. Think about how you live your life from day to day. In what ways do you ever act like you are worshipping an unknown God? In what ways do you acknowledge that "in him we live and move and have our being"?

Your life is a gift from God. You didn't earn it, or deserve it. Neither did I. We'r
not so good, so intelligent, or so attractive that God was forced to provide us wit
life. That life is his gift to us—that alone is worth a thousand lifetimes of gratitud
Even more incredible is the fact that the Lord longs for a relationship with us. An
yet we often fill our moments with things that have nothing to do with him.

We pass our days in activities and with attitudes that often suggest we don
even know who he is. Let's make it our goal today to cherish what God has give
us—the opportunity to know and be known by the creator of the universe. He ha
made it all possible; now it's your move!

YOUR↗SPIN

Regarding your priorities, see if the following statements are
true or false.

1. _____ I struggle to find time to pray, and when I do I
don't know what to say.

2. _____ I prefer to read the daily news over God's Word.

3. _____ I am bored in a worship service—I can't seem to
focus on God.

4. _____ I would rather do something for others than meditate
on God.

5. _____ I like giving to God; tithing my income is never an
effort.

It's Your Move!

If God is indeed relational, then he wants a relationship with all people, especially those who don't know him yet. Though he is not far from any of us, some will meet him best through an association with you. What are you doing to create new bonds with those who aren't Christians?

How well do you know your neighbors? When is the last time you did more than just wave over the fence? Look for someone in your neighborhood to befriend; through that growing relationship you may have the opportunity to share what a difference Jesus has made in your life.

As a small group look for ways you can reach out to the spiritually apathetic through no-strings-attached deeds of kindness.

- Do you know an elderly couple who could use some home repair?

- How about being a Big Brother or Big Sister to a teenager looking for a positive influence?

- Undoubtedly there is a single parent nearby who could use your help.

Don't view these individuals as projects; view them as potential new friends in your life. If they become a friend, you will be blessed and hopefully they will discover a lasting relationship with the Lord through you.

BONUS

Want to be a winner in the game of life? Then build a relationship with the one who knows the road—he said it best, "I am the way, the truth, and the LIFE!"

POINT

CLUE:

Discovering the Whole Truth

PART ONE—GAME ON

Object of the Game

A murder has occurred, and you're the private investigator that is assigned to the case. But *which* guest did it, and *what* did he use to accomplish the dastardly deed and *where* did it actually happen? And what will you learn about truth as you investigate your way through the game?

Game Preparation

You will need at least two game boards so that everyone in the group can play; more if your group is larger than twelve (unless you want to team up). If you are short on time and have Internet access, go to the following Web site to play the CLUE game in a virtual view: http://www.hasbro.com/clue/content/virtual-mansion/index.html. To enhance this Web-based edition, connect your computer to a large-screen television or digital projector. You'll feel as if you've stepped into the crime scene.

> "Always tell the truth. You may make a hole-in-one when you're alone on the golf course someday."
>
> —Franklin P. Jones

Use a little creativity for this group event. Whoever is hosting the small group might want to consider decorating with a mystery theme: magnifying glasses, fingerprint cards at every table place, phony FBI badges, a chunk of dry ice in water to provide a low fog—think mysteriously. Each member of the small group could come dressed as his or her favorite CLUE character or famous fictional detective.

Before the game begins, see who scores the highest on this TV/movie detectives quiz. Match the character with the actor who played the role:

- Inspector Clouseau
- Perry Mason
- Jessica Fletcher
- Gil Grissom
- Magnum PI
- Jim Rockford
- Jill Munroe
- Sergeant Joe Friday
- Lilly Rush
- Columbo
- Kojak
- Brenda Leigh Johnson

- William Petersen
- Kyra Sedgwick
- Tom Selleck
- Kathryn Morris
- Peter Sellers
- Telly Savalas
- Peter Falk
- Raymond Burr
- Farrah Fawcett
- James Garner
- Jack Webb
- Angela Lansbury

TRIVIA

*T*he CLUE game is a classic Parker Brothers/Hasbro board game that has transitioned through several updates and is now marketed to new generations of fans in forty different countries around the world. The fictitious murder of Mr. John Boddy in his palatial mansion is the setting—a mystery that translates well into any culture. The popularity of the game has not only spawned numerous versions, but also inspired a 1985 movie and a 1997 musical of the same name. The movie (available on DVD) has three different endings to choose from, and the musical involved the whole audience in solving the crime. I doubt that retired clerk Anthony E. Pratt could have imagined such success when he and his wife first developed the game Cluedo in their simple English home during World War II (http://www.hasbro.com/clue/default.cfm?page=History). Parker Brothers immediately bought the rights and began marketing the U.S. version of the CLUE game in 1949 with real rope as one of the weapons (Bruce Whitehill, Games—American Boxed Games and their Makers 1822-1992, Wallace-Homestead: Radnor, Pennsylvania, 1992, p. 27).

Suggesting that "it was Colonel Mustard in the billiard room with the lead pipe" is only one of 324 possible solutions. One mystery, however, remains unsolved—no one knows why Mr. Boddy was murdered.

Playing by the Rules

Eliminating the possible suspects, rooms, and murder weapons is the challenge. you can be the first to narrow down the possibilities and make an allegation, you' likely come away the winner. Playing by the rules is exciting enough, but if you war to add some intrigue of your own, try one of these variations.

Play as two-person teams. One team member always rolls the dice and decide which direction to move; the other team member asks all the probing question and takes notes.

Another approach is to assign various rooms in the house to represent the room of the game. Where one would normally move a game piece from room to room o the board, *each person* moves from room to room in the house. The dice determine the number of normal steps each player can take to reach the various rooms. Onc in the center of the selected room, a player can make a Suggestion, parts of whic can then be proven or disproven. Since every player will need to be in the room t hear the Suggestion, make color markers (e.g., six different color sheets of pape weighted color balloons, etc.) to leave behind so that players can return to their las locations before their next turns. The game ends when one of the players correctl makes an Accusation, identifying the three cards in the Case File.

It also might be fun to encourage players to get into their roles and to feel fre to elaborate on their story lines, dropping hints to cause confusion along the way

To Eat

Have each group member or family bring a dish that reflects one of the suspect in the CLUE detective game. Col. Mustard might bring deviled eggs since tha spicy condiment is used in those yummy, yellow treats. Here are a few othe idea starters:

- Mr. Green—spinach dip
- Mrs. White—angel food cake
- Miss Scarlet—tart cherry pie
- Prof. Plum—fresh plums
- Mrs. Peacock—chicken salad sandwiches

Perhaps your group would like to share a mystery meal before the game begins. This will take a little extra time, but it will be worth it. The host decides upon the menu and members help to bring the food, but the host gives every meal item a mysterious name, including the eating utensils and beverages, if you like. For instance, the spoon might be called "magnifying glass" and the knife "pathologist's helper." A slice of bread could be named "fingerprint card." You get the picture. Everyone orders in courses: appetizer, salad, main course, and dessert. You can only order four items per course, and you must fill out the entire order before anything is served. You might get the dessert for an appetizer or not get your fork, spoon, or knife until the last course, but you must eat whatever you are served in that course. It will be removed when the next course arrives. Since only the host and hostess know the code, they participate by serving and watching the fun.

For Younger Players

For the children in your small group, look for a CLUE, Jr. Edition game and let them play at their own pace. There is also a version of the game for the computer that kids will really enjoy. Or, have the kids dress up as the CLUE characters and play as your partners. Or hide mystery items or clues throughout the meeting space and have the kids go on a scavenger hunt. As the game progresses, ask the children (and the adults!) these questions:

- Why it is important to keep searching for the truth?

- How does looking at evidence help us discover the truth?

- Why should we be honest?

Picking Up the Pieces

When the religious leaders brought Jesus before Pilate and accused him of treasonous crimes worthy of death, Pilate responded to Jesus' declaration about his kingdom, "You are a king, then!" Jesus answered him, "You are right in saying I am a king. In fact, for this reason I was born, and for this I came into the world, to testify to the truth. Everyone on the side of truth listens to me." "What is truth?" Pilate asked, as he went back out to the Jews (John 18:37, 38).

"Truth isn't always beauty, but the hunger for it is."

—Nadine Gordimer, "A Bolter and the Invincible Summer," *London Magazine*, May 1963

TAKE 🎲 TURNS

After the mystery has been solved, take a few minutes to investigate and examine these inquiring thoughts:

1. Do you relish the thought of searching through evidence and digging for truth, or do you find that activity dull and meaningless? Explain.

2. Define *truth*. Is there such a thing as absolute truth?

3. Who gets to say what truth is or isn't?

How would you have answered Pilate's question? What did Jesus mean when he said, "Everyone on the side of truth listens to me"?

Make a list of the top five quests for truth in our culture. Discuss ways a genuine seeker can find the answers. End your session by praying that God will give you more:

• honesty in seeking truth.

• clarity in discerning truth.

• humility in knowing truth.

CLUE:
Discovering the Whole Truth

PART TWO—POSTGAME BREAKDOWN

Object of the Study

Feeling like a competent detective after a round of the CLUE game? What did you learn from a trip through the mysterious mansion? I'm sure you know digging for the truth isn't just about winning a game. Let's discover what truth we need to know to be a winner in life.

Bible Content

Reading the entire text of Ecclesiastes is recommended for this session. However, if that isn't possible, read the following selected passages from this book of divine wisdom.

> *"Meaningless! Meaningless!" says the Teacher. "Utterly meaningless! Everything is meaningless." What does man gain from all his labor at which he toils under the sun? Generations come and generations go, but the earth remains forever. . . . All things are wearisome, more than one can say. The eye never has enough of seeing, nor the ear its fill of hearing. What has been will be again, what has been done will be done again; there is nothing new under the sun. . . . What a heavy burden God has laid on men! I have seen all the things that are done under the sun; all of them are meaningless, a chasing after the wind.*
>
> —Ecclesiastes 1:2-4, 8, 9, 13, 14

To Study

In an odd sort of way, life corresponds to a CLUE game. Mysteries surround us. Everything is suspect. Can anyone be trusted? In a time when the concept of absolute truth is dismissed as unattainable, we long for steadfast, reliable answers to life's most probing questions. We want truth!

Radio Shack once advertised with the slogan, "You've got questions; we've got answers." Long before we had radios, or shacks, for that matter, God invited us to find in him the answers for our deepest longings.

In Ecclesiastes the wise King Solomon writes about his quest for purpose and meaning in life. His journal, written in his later years, begins with the musings of one who was as clueless as we are but who had every opportunity to find the truth. So grab your detective's notebook and let's do some investigating.

TAKE TURNS

1. Did you ever make a purchase or otherwise obtain something you thought would bring satisfaction, only to discover it brought frustration? What happened?

2. List some other ways we seek contentment in life. What nagging questions do we seek answers to?

3. What do you know about Solomon? Why do you think the wise king was so restless? Can you relate?

Think about three questions that you would like to find true answers for.

1. What have you done to find these answers? Where have you looked?

2. What do you think finding out the truth will do for you?

3. Have you asked God for help in finding out the truth? Do you think you can be content even if you don't get the answers you want? Why or why not?

PASS THE GUILT

Play the CLUE game long enough and each of the player-suspects will turn up as the guilty party in the evidence envelope. That's life in a nutshell—we all are guilty! Not an innocent person among us. We stand before God guilty as charged.

Do you know how it started? In the words of a zealous CLUE detective, it was: Satan, in the Garden, with forbidden fruit. Both Adam and Eve fell prey to a deadly twisting of truth; and sin, with its ugly consequences, entered the world with a bite. I hope it was sweet, because the aftertaste sure is bitter. Not long afterwards it was: Cain, in the field, with a rock or club or his bare hands. The blood of his murdered brother Abel cried out from the ground for justice. The world went from bad to worse. A fresh start was needed, so at the right time it was: God, in the heavens, with a global flood.

The answers we long to know will continue to elude us until we grasp the truth of our guilt. Ever since that episode in Eden, humanity has been in rebellion against God (Romans 3:23). Understanding that truth is foundational to any knowledge we have of ourselves and God.

CLUE

How did Solomon set about to discover truth? One might say he used the elimination method—he explored every adventure available to him in an effort to find the truth.

- *Solomon the partier.* Given his lofty position as king, Solomon spared no expense in seeking out the best food and entertainment money could buy. The laughter faded quickly and hunger always returned the following day (see Ecclesiastes 2:1-3).

- *Solomon the builder.* With seemingly unlimited resources, the king built houses, farmed the fields, cultivated vineyards, dug reservoirs, created parks, and planted gardens. If it could be built or harvested, he tried it. It was a chasing after the wind (see 2:4-6, 11).

- *Solomon the spender.* With all of his wealth, Solomon could own or be treated to the best of the best: clothes of the richest fabrics, exquisite palace furnishings, world-class sculptures and artwork, private performances in the palace, a four-chariot garage, vacations to exotic coastal towns, and any book or scroll available. Another empty pursuit (see 5:10).

- *Solomon the diplomat.* Thinking that purpose and meaning rested upon the alliances and treaties he could negotiate, Solomon implored surrounding nations to find peace together. His contribution was to marry the princesses of those lands! Still, he felt empty (see 1 Kings 11:1-3).

TAKE TURNS

1. What do you think is more harmful: distorted truth or ignored truth? How has either of those hurt you or someone you know?

2. When you read that everyone is a sinner, does that strike you first as being true about yourself? Or do you think of other sinners first? Why?

3. How can understanding and admitting our guilt help us find truth?

YOUR SPIN

Pretend for a moment you're creating a game called Clueless. The rooms might include a computer room linked in to pornographic Web sites and sordid chat networks or a windowless study where crooked business deals are hatched. What other rooms might you create for Clueless? What activities, events, or places could potentially destroy your character and distract you from the truth?

- *Solomon the collector.* If one is good, then many are better, so the king added to his collection: household servants, flocks, herds, singers, silver, gold, and wives. Yes, you read it correctly; he collected wives—seven hundred to be exact! (Was he really all that wise?)

- *Solomon the laborer.* Since signing edicts and laws wasn't energizing enough, Solomon tried manual labor. He worked hard at a variety of projects, but in the end his toil only produced sore muscles (see Ecclesiastes 2:17-19).

- *Solomon the student.* In exercising his brain, Solomon discovered that wisdom was better than folly, but not much. In the end both the wise and foolish take up residence in the grave.

Israel's king summed it up this way: "I denied myself nothing my eyes desired; I refused my heart no pleasure. . . . Yet when I surveyed all that my hands had done and what I had toiled to achieve, everything was meaningless, a chasing after the wind" (Ecclesiastes 2:10, 11).

Unfortunately, we, like Solomon, often spend our lives searching for meaning. Some scuba dive while others skydive, but the intent is the same—to find a pursuit that will satisfy our restless souls. Be careful where you go in search of that contentment; some destinations will destroy your character, if not your life. Some stones are better left unturned.

CLUE   39

Ecclesiastes, for some, is a rather pessimistic take on life. But actually, Solomon takes a realistic approach and arrives at some surprising conclusions. For instance, logic would suggest that the race will be won by the fastest runner or the battle will be won by the most powerful army. Such is not always the case (see Ecclesiastes 9:11). In a perfect world, such logic might prevail, but this world is far from perfect. It's broken! When Sin showed up in Eden, he brought along his cousins Destruction, Decay, and Death.

- In a broken world the playing field isn't level.

- In a broken world life isn't fair.

- In a broken world peace is elusive and hope is lost.

- In a broken world disease and destitution have the upper hand.

- In a broken world bad things happen to good people.

In a broken world many things are beyond our control. The truth is—nothing in a broken world can fill the emptiness in our broken lives. That's what Solomon discovered and why he writes to warn us. He searched for truth in every possible place and found it in only one source. It's as if Solomon has interviewed every player, visited every room, and examined every conceivable weapon before drawing his conclusion. If you are expecting some new clue, some profound insight into the mysterious meaning of life, you might be surprised. When Solomon pulled the cards out of the confidential envelope, this is the answer he discovered: "Now all has been heard; here is the conclusion of the matter: Fear God and keep his commandments, for this is the whole duty of man. For God will bring every deed into judgment, including every hidden thing, whether it is good or evil" (Ecclesiastes 12:13, 14).

TAKE TURNS

1. When someone asks how a loving God could let bad things happen to good people, how do you answer?

2. Is truth created or discovered? What's the difference?

That's it.

- Respect God—develop healthy fear of God's awesome nature and power.

- Obey God—follow his counsel and commands; this is our duty as created beings and as children of God.

- Answer to God—in the final analysis we are only accountable to God, no one else. And without the Lord, you don't have a clue!

The complete revelation of God's truth came a millennium after Solomon. The mystery was solved, once and for all, in the most incredible event of history. Only God knew how it would begin—it was: Judas, in Gethsemane, with a kiss. From Peter's denial to Pilate's dilemma, the pieces of God's mystery began to come together. And for all of us, the guilty, God left no stone unturned. What had been squandered in Eden, he bought back. The price? It was: Jesus, at Calvary, with the cross.

It's Your Move!

Someday we will answer to God for our actions and intentions in this world. Since staying on the straight and narrow is difficult when you are traveling alone, developing a system of personal accountability is a must. Here is your assignment:

- Determine one or two people you can trust with your innermost secrets and concerns. They may be in your small group but that isn't necessary.

- Ask them to help you stay on target spiritually. Determine when you could meet together regularly so that each of you can hold one another accountable in his or her relationship with God.

- Compose a list of six meaningful but tough questions that will cut to the core of your struggles.

- Close each accountability meeting with a prayer time.

Some get stuck in their limited knowledge of the world and stop searching for the whole truth. A winner realizes early on that the whole truth is revealed through a relationship with Jesus Christ. That truth will "set you free."

SORRY:
Finding the Freedom of Forgiveness

PART ONE—GAME ON

Object of the Game

Playing the SORRY! board game will challenge your ability to control both your resentment and your desire for revenge. Take careful note of your attitudes as you round the board and head for home. A forgiving spirit makes the game more palatable.

Game Preparation

The SORRY! game is for two to four players, so you can either break your group into four teams or collect enough games so everyone has a spot around a board. Before anyone draws the first action card from the shuffled deck, take some time to chat about these thoughts. Begin with the youngest in the group.

> "I've had a few arguments with people, but I never carry a grudge. You know why? While you' carrying a grudge, they'r out dancing."
>
> —Buddy Hackett, comedian

- When was the last time you said "I'm sorry" to a stranger? When was the last time you said those words to a friend? Which experience was harder? Why?

- Why do most people struggle with saying "I'm sorry"? Are these words difficult for you to repeat?

- Which do you think is easier: to hold onto a grudge or let it go? Explain your answer.

The SORRY! game was first marketed in the United States in 1934 and since that time has become a family favorite. The earliest variation of the game can be traced back to England, when William Henry Storey of Southend-on-Sea applied for a patent in 1929, but its game play style is actually centuries old. The board game evolved out of a family of games called Cross and Circle, developed in India five hundred years before the birth of Christ. Play involves moving one's markers around spaces on a circle or cross, with the goal to be the first to safely move one's pawns all the way around the board. In ancient times royalty played the game with beautifully costumed dancers on giant outdoor game boards. The oldest known version is called pachisi or, as it is better known in North America, Parcheesi (taken from http://en.wikipedia.org/wiki/Parcheesi, March 2, 2009).

The modern-day SORRY! game is a chase where players constantly bump, switch, and slide their way home. Filled with backward and forward moves and that special SORRY! card, which can send your unhappy opponent all the way back to start, the game tests every player in the area of self-control. In his original British patent (no. GB339653), William Storey described the game as having been "proved by experience to be a prolific source of amusement."

Playing by the Rules

Game play involves moving all four of your markers or pawns around the board from start to home. If time allows, follow the general rules of the game and play it to its conclusion. However, if time is limited, here are a few options to consider:

- Shuffle the deck and deal out all of the cards. You only go through the cards once, so the person who has the most pawns in home base when the cards are exhausted wins.

- Play with only one pawn for each player instead of four. This is the SORRY! sudden death version. The first player to get his pawn safely to home base wins.

- Play a tournament. For this adaptation you will need a timer and a score-keeper for each match. Each game will be limited to fifteen minutes. When the timer goes off, the players with the highest and lowest point totals for that round each move to another match. Points are scored as follows: five points for every pawn in home circle; three points for every pawn in the safe zone; one point for pawns on the board; minus two points for every pawn still in start when the game concludes. The tournament will consist of four rounds. At the end of the tournament the points from all four matches are tallied and the player with the most total points wins.

- If you really want to put forgiveness to the test, try a round with these rules. Shuffle the deck and place it facedown. Each player draws a card. This continues until someone draws a SORRY! card. This player becomes the Grudge. The Grudge then selects a number card (not one dedicated to some unique purpose), which when drawn by any other player automatically sends his pawn back to the start and costs the player an extra turn. Only the Grudge is exempt and can use the number card as originally intended. The rest of the general rules apply.

To Eat

Since this lesson involves hot tempers and refreshing forgiveness, offer a variety of spicy and cool treats. Here are a few suggestions:

- Small bowls of Red Hots candies scattered about.

- A platter of hot wings or Buffalo wings. If you serve more than one level of spicy wings, label their increasing heat index with such words as Mildly Offensive, Irritating, Infuriating, Appalling, and Unforgivable. Use your imagination.

- A variety of flavored chips such as jalapeño, spicy BBQ, and cool ranch.

- For something refreshing, try a platter of fresh fruit. Or offer a Forgiveness Is Sweet Bar—a selection of frozen yogurt or ice cream and all the toppings.

"Forgiveness is a funny thing. It warms the heart and cools the sting."

—William Arthur Ward, American inspirational writer

For Younger Players

For younger players in your small group, you can provide a kids' version of the classic game. There is even a SORRY! game edition for Gameboy Advance.

For even younger children in the group, let them play as your partners. They can be responsible for moving each pawn as you read the card. Use various moves on the board to teach valuable lessons on anger and forgiveness:

- Card #4—"Back up four spaces." Often when we grow angry we lose something: it could be a friend, a chance to be happy, or the respect of someone we love.

- When your pawn is almost home and is suddenly sent back to the start by one of the other players, talk about disappointment. Discuss different (good and bad) ways people handle disappointment and how we can channel frustration in positive directions.

TAKE TURNS

As the last pawn slides safely into home, discuss these questions:

1. How frustrating was your SORRY! round? Which parts of the game did you enjoy or dislike the most?

2. How did you react when another player sent your pawn back to the start? How did attitudes toward the game or toward each other change as the game progressed?

Picking Up the Pieces

I'm sorry—simple words that are difficult to speak. Concluding that I am at fault is not difficult; admitting it out loud is another story. I suspect you may feel the same. And if seeking forgiveness is painful, extending it to someone who has offended you can be excruciating. For that very reason we truly need the Lord's help to genuinely forgive one another.

- Read Matthew 5:23, 24—How is your giving to God impacted by your willingness to seek forgiveness from one you have offended?

- Read Matthew 6:14, 15—How are your prayers for forgiveness impacted by your willingness to forgive those who have offended you?

Close by praying the Lord's Prayer together (Matthew 6:9-13).

SORRY:

Finding the Freedom of Forgiveness

PART TWO—POSTGAME BREAKDOWN

Object of the Study

Now that your tempers have cooled and your frustrations have subsided, let's explore what Jesus had to say about the necessity of forgiveness.

Bible Content

We all want the Lord to think the best of us and our motives. I'm confident that was Peter's goal when he posed his question to Jesus in such a curious manner.

> Then Peter came to Jesus and asked, "Lord, how many times shall I forgive my brother when he sins against me? Up to seven times?"
>
> Jesus answered, "I tell you, not seven times, but seventy-seven times.
>
> "Therefore, the kingdom of heaven is like a king who wanted to settle accounts with his servants. As he began the settlement, a man who owed him ten thousand talents was brought to him. Since he was not able to pay, the master ordered that he and his wife and his children and all that he had be sold to repay the debt.
>
> "The servant fell on his knees before him. 'Be patient with me,' he begged, 'and I will pay back everything.' The servant's master took pity on him, canceled the debt and let him go.
>
> "But when that servant went out, he found one of his fellow servants who owed him a hundred denarii. He grabbed him and began to choke him. 'Pay back what you owe me!' he demanded.
>
> "His fellow servant fell to his knees and begged him, 'Be patient with me, and I will pay you back.'
>
> "But he refused. Instead, he went off and had the man thrown into prison until he could pay the debt. When the other servants saw what had happened, they were greatly distressed

and went and told their master everything that had happened.

"Then the master called the servant in. 'You wicked servant,' he said, 'I canceled all that debt of yours because you begged me to. Shouldn't you have had mercy on your fellow servant just as I had on you?' In anger his master turned him over to the jailers to be tortured, until he should pay back all he owed.

"This is how my heavenly Father will treat each of you unless you forgive your brother from your heart."

—Matthew 18:21-35

To Study

Love Story, the 1970 Hollywood adaptation of Shakespeare's *Romeo and Juliet*, produced a classic line—"Love means never having to say you're sorry." What an idiotic statement! True love willingly apologizes and seeks for ways to forgive.

A LIFE-CHALLENGING QUESTION: "HOW MANY TIMES MUST I FORGIVE?"

In Peter's day the accepted norm was to forgive an individual three times. That traditional view may have developed from the writings of the prophet Amos, when he employed this bit of prose to emphasize his point: "For three transgressions and for four . . ." (Amos 1, 2). Here's how the scholars of the day reached their conclusion: If God's forgiveness extended to three offenses and divine judgment followed on the fourth, then no human should be more gracious than God. Therefore, God's people are bound only to forgive three times.

TAKE TURNS

1. Have you ever been routinely offended or insulted by the same person? What do you do to keep the attitude of forgiveness fresh?

2. How can we reconcile the need to forgive multiple times with the fear of becoming a doormat or pushover?

3. Have you ever been the repeat offender? Was it difficult for you to apologize multiple times?

Take an inventory of your forgiveness factor. Rate the following statements with an N for never, an S for sometimes, or an O for often.

1. I say I forgive, but then it takes me several days (or longer) to feel like talking to that person again. _____

2. I forgive readily before a person asks, and put the episode out of my mind as soon as possible. _____

3. I forgive readily when someone asks, but I keep a record of the event in my head and bring it up later if I have cause. _____

4. I feel better about myself and the situation if I forgive the offender right away. _____

Look over your answers. How do you feel about where you are with forgiveness? How can you get better at forgiving people?

Knowing that background you can better understand Peter's approach. The crusty fisherman-turned-disciple was beginning to catch a glimpse of the concept of grace—he was willing to go way beyond the legalistic expectations of the day. Why seven times? Perhaps he understood the number seven to be a biblical number of completeness—and if anything needs to be complete, it is forgiveness.

It is debatable whether Jesus meant seventy-seven times or seven times seventy (490). In actuality it makes no difference; the lesson is the same—forgiveness knows no limitations.

A LIFE-CHANGING ANSWER: "FORGIVE YOUR BROTHER FROM YOUR HEART."

Jesus' answer knocked the props right out from under Peter. I suspect Peter was waiting for a pat on the back for his generous suggestion, but Jesus' response came more like a kick in the pants. With Peter once again humbled, Jesus used the occasion to teach about forgiveness.

The answer also humbles us. I don't know anyone who finds forgiveness easy. If you are human, forgiveness is a struggle. And taken at face value, Jesus' answer begs another question or two.

- Is he suggesting that I must forgive everyone who does me wrong? Yes.

- What if they don't apologize; what if they don't ask to be forgiven? The answer remains the same.

Don't miss this truth—we forgive to be like God, not because someone deserves our forgiveness. Deserving forgiveness is not a part of the equation. If it were, none of us would ever be forgiven. The ability to forgive sets one apart from the average person. Is it easy? No way. Is it the right thing to do? Absolutely! Will you feel better as a result? I guarantee it!

A LIFE-REFLECTING PARABLE: "SHOULDN'T YOU HAVE HAD MERCY?"

If the answer of Jesus leaves any doubt, his parable draws a picture that is undeniably clear. We feel a sense of utter disdain for the ungrateful debtor who was forgiven a humongous debt (think of it as our national debt) but could not find it in himself to forgive a pittance from a fellow debtor. We cheer at the just conclusion of the story. But before we can don the party hats and toss the confetti, the overwhelming truth dawns on each of us—*I am that debtor.*

Consider the two actions necessary to bring a happy resolution to the story, and to our stories. The first is *apologizing*. Some people just can't bring themselves to apologize. They will smile, slap you on the back, tell you what a good friend you are, and act as if nothing ever happened, but you will not hear them utter the words, "I am sorry." Do you know what I've discovered? People admire those who can admit wrong and act contrite. Every human being needs to learn how to apologize.

Spiritually, an apology to God is called repentance, which means a change of mind that leads to a change of behavior. Repentance is recognizing one's failure

IT'S YOUR MOVE—ON BOARD

to keep God's commands and is vital to our forgiveness. Jesus said, "But unless you repent, you too will all perish" (Luke 13:3).

Repentance requires that we acknowledge our sin. A quotation I once saw had a good take on this: "Confession without repentance is just bragging" (attributed to Rev. Eugene Bolton). Our politically correct society has determined that the concept of sin is offensive. No one should call another's behavior wrong. And no one should tell another person what he or she ought to do to make it right.

As Christians we are held to a higher standard than what society demands. God's Word clearly distinguishes between right and wrong, and when we are wrong there is but one right response he will accept—genuine repentance. "He who conceals his sins does not prosper, but whoever confesses and renounces them finds mercy" (Proverbs 28:13).

YOUR ↗ SPIN

Consider these practical ways to help improve your ability to apologize. Rank them in order of their importance to you.

_____ Pray—if you struggle to apologize, ask God to change your attitude.

_____ Practice the Golden Rule—if you want others to admit their faults and apologize to you, you must learn to do the same.

_____ Partner with a trusted friend—be accountable. This is not about sharing gossip but learning from one who will help point out your need to apologize.

_____ Prepare your apology—write out your apology and read it aloud. If you struggle to verbalize an apology, practice on the family canine. Even the dog will love you more!

TAKE TURNS

1. Why do we find repentance so uncomfortable?

2. List some ways you can improve your prayers of repentance.

3. Why do you suppose God commanded us not to seek revenge?

4. How can you forgive someone who hasn't apologized or, worse yet, doesn't care that he or she has inflicted pain in your life? How can you make the decision to forgive?

The second action, and the much more challenging one for most, is *forgiving*. Forgiveness, the true theme of this parable, is not something you can truly appreciate apart from experiencing the forgiveness of God in your own life.

- Forgiveness is not a feeling; if it were we would never get it done. Who *feels* like forgiving?

- Forgiveness is not to be equated with forgetting. Whoever penned the words "forgive and forget" was clueless about human nature. We cannot erase the hard drive of the brain. Painful deeds leveled against us never leave us.

- Forgiveness is not excusing another's behavior as if to give the perpetrator a pass. It is not letting someone off the hook or eliminating the consequence of his actions. The guilty party is still at fault.

- Forgiveness is a decision. Such responses as:
  > withholding our forgiveness,
  > continually dwelling on the wrong,
  > broadcasting the wrong through gossip,
  > seeking revenge against the guilty,

  will exact a high price from you in the long run. Some wise sage wrote, "Unforgiveness is the poison we drink hoping others will die."

But what if the offender does not apologize? Ideally, a repentant attitude should precede forgiveness, but when it is absent we still must forgive. Here then is the bottom line: forgiveness is truly for your benefit. Forgiveness lifts your burden, buries your grudge, and strengthens your relationship to the Lord.

It's Your Move!

Have each person bring a note card and envelope—write either a note of apology or a note of forgiveness. The note can be addressed to a family member, friend, coworker, or casual acquaintance. You will be surprised how this simple act can advance the healing process in a relationship that needs repair.

William Stoddard wrote: "Forgiving the unforgivable is hard. So was the cross: hard words, hard wood, hard nails." If God has lavished us with such forgiveness, how can we refuse to forgive those who offend us?

CANDY LAND:
Tasting and Seeing God's Goodness

PART ONE—GAME ON

Object of the Game

The CANDY LAND board game might be easy to play, but that's not to suggest the lesson it illustrates is any less significant. As you travel around the colorful board, perhaps a detour through Chocolate Swamp or a stop at the Candy Castle will help sweeten your disposition. More importantly, throughout this activity I hope you will taste and see God's goodness.

Game Preparation

The classic version of the CANDY LAND game will be fun for all ages, but you are certainly not limited to only one option. Hasbro also offers popular cartoon character versions of the game. For even more entertainment you could show *Candy Land: the Great Lollipop Adventure* available in VHS or DVD format, or you can combine the best of both worlds and interact electronically with the CANDY LAND DVD Game. And as you might expect there is also an interactive CD-ROM version of this colorful board game for use on computers.

> "It's not true that nice guys finish last. Nice guys are winner before the game even starts."
>
> —Addison Walker

Four players or teams can play the game at one time, so you may need to borrow a couple more boards for use with your group. Or, if you wanted to go really outside the box, you could make a CANDY LAND game trail that wound its way around your meeting room or throughout the host's house. You could use sheets of construction paper for the game board squares and paste them on cardboard or posterboard—the same concept would work for the game cards.

Setting the mood for this young-at-heart activity could include homemade posters of the various CANDY LAND game characters: Gramma Nut, Mamma Gingertree, Mr. Mint, Princess Frostine, etc.

Each group member or family could bring a game-related decoration: a gumdrop mountain, a gingerbread (or graham cracker) house, a peppermint stick forest, a lollipop woods, a peanut field, and, my favorite, a chocolate swamp. Design them so part of the decoration can also be enjoyed as a tasty treat.

TRIVIA

This story starts in 1940, in a land called California, in a not very fun place called the hospital, where Eleanor Abbot, thirty years old, lay recovering from a disease called polio. Feeling sympathy for all the children around her also recovering from the effects of the disease, Eleanor got the idea for a simple but delightful children's game. She created an imaginative adventure through a land of various candy delights. She submitted her board game to the Milton Bradley Company, who recognized its value and began production in 1949. The first CANDY LAND games sold for only a dollar, and the advertisements assured parents that the game fulfilled "the sweet-tooth yearning of the younger set without the tummy ache aftereffects." While I doubt any sweet-tooth craving was spared, the game did catch on quickly and has become one of the most celebrated children's board games of all time. Eleanor Abbot could never have predicted that her sweet idea created through the difficulties of a bitter disease would someday sell over forty million games (http://www.hasbro.com/candyland/en_US/discover/history.cfm).

The game has changed some: Molasses Swamp is now Chocolate Swamp, Queen Frostine has been demoted to Princess, and Plumpy has been banished from the game board. Even so, the CANDY LAND game continues to be a popular family favorite.

Playing by the Rules

Since this game is designed for children of all ages, it would be good to stick to the simple rules during play, if you are planning on playing with the children in your group. This activity is intended to be more about inclusiveness than cleverness.

If the children in your small group are older, if you don't have any, or if they are playing separately, you may consider tweaking the rules a bit. Use a single die (in place of the cards) to determine spaces moved. Require additional activity when a player lands on specially designated color squares. Here are some possibilities to consider:

- Land on red—move back two squares.
- Land on purple—move ahead one square.
- Land on yellow—lose a turn.
- Land on blue—exchange places with another player farther down the path.
- Land on green—eat a piece of candy.

Choose your own designations and make the game more interesting for your group.

To Eat

Wow! The food options are nearly unlimited for this activity:

- Gingerbread Men (or Boy and Girl) cookies.
- Tree-shaped frosted Sugar Cookies with sprinkles.
- A platter of peanuts or mixed nuts.
- A bowl of mixed candy—gumdrops, chocolate pieces, peppermints, and licorice sticks.
- Gelatin Rainbow—mix up different fruity flavors of gelatin mixes, and add them layer by layer to a glass dish, cooling each layer before adding the next one.

In order to avoid a sugar high, offer some healthier options as well:

- Veggie Island (tray of chopped carrots, broccoli, celery, cauliflower, etc.) with a Ranch Dip Swamp.
- Frozen fruit juice pops.
- Fruity Formal Gardens—a fruit pizza (recipe on next page).

For Younger Players

You won't have to work hard to include kids in this game. They can play their own CANDY LAND game or join in with the adults. However, if you need some other activities for them, Hasbro also offers related CANDY LAND character online games (if you have a computer you don't mind the kids using) and has coloring pages you can print out. Go to www.hasbro.com, search for CANDY LAND, and then look under the "Play Candy Land" heading.

And here is a simple learning activity. Tell the kids that the original versions of the game had Molasses Swamp instead of Chocolate Swamp. Hasbro made this

CRUST:

½ CUP BUTTER, SOFTENED

¾ CUP WHITE SUGAR

1 EGG

1 ¼ CUPS ALL-PURPOSE FLOUR

1 TEASPOON CREAM OF TARTAR

½ TEASPOON BAKING SODA

¼ TEASPOON SALT

FILLING:

1 (8 OUNCE) PACKAGE CREAM CHEESE

½ CUP WHITE SUGAR

2 TEASPOONS VANILLA EXTRACT

TOPPING:

FRUIT OF CHOICE

Preheat oven to 350 degrees F (175 degrees C). Cream together the butter and ¾ cup sugar until smooth. Beat in egg. Combine the flour, cream of tartar, baking soda, and salt; stir the flour mixture gradually into the creamed mixture until just blended. Press dough into an ungreased pizza pan. Bake in preheated oven for 8 to 10 minutes, or until lightly browned. Cool.

In a large bowl, mix cream cheese with ½ cup sugar and vanilla until well mixed and beat the mixture until it is light. Spread cream cheese filling on cooled crust.

Arrange fruit of your choice on top of filling to make a pleasant display, and chill. Some suggestions for fruit: blueberries, raspberries, strawberries, kiwi, banana, peach slices, and fresh pineapple slices. Think about how you want to arrange the colors before you start, and make sure the fruit pieces are dry before you place them on the filling. You can sprinkle lemon juice over cut banana and apple slices to keep them from turning brown before serving. Makes about 10 servings, but it depends on how you wish to slice it.

change because most children today don't know what molasses is. Provide a small jar of molasses and plastic spoons. Let everyone have a taste. Ask the kids: Which one tastes sweeter, molasses or chocolate? What about molasses or chocolate reminds you of God's goodness? (It's something you crave, it sticks to us, etc.)

If the kids haven't heard it, take time to read the Legend of Lost Candy Castle, printed on the game box.

Picking Up the Pieces

King David, the man after God's own heart, wrote in Psalm 34:8: "Taste and see that the LORD is good; blessed is the man who takes refuge in him."

- Life looks different through the eyes of a child; in a broken world how do you communicate the goodness of God?

- Make a list of God's good qualities. What does David mean when he says "taste and see"? How does one do that; how can you taste the goodness of God?

- When the media seems to emphasize the bad news, what steps can we take to focus on the good news? How can we keep our eyes focused on God?

Take time to pray together. Ask God to help you to:

- seek his goodness in this world.

- know more about his goodness in this world.

- be a reflection of his goodness in this world.

TAKE TURNS

1. Does playing Candy Land bring back memories from your childhood? What are your favorite memories from your preschool or kindergarten years?

2. What do you miss from those early years of life?

3. As a child, were you able to see more goodness in the world than you do as an adult? Explain your answer.

CANDY LAND:
Tasting and Seeing God's Goodness

PART TWO—POSTGAME BREAKDOWN

Object of the Study

After your tasty trip through Gumdrop Pass and Chocolate Swamp, consider these spiritual lessons that will help you through the highs and lows of life.

Bible Content

> Taste and see that the LORD is good; blessed is the man who takes refuge in him.
>
> —Psalm 34:8

> And we know that in all things God works for the good of those who love him, who have been called according to his purpose.
>
> —Romans 8:28

> I have kept my feet from every evil path
> so that I might obey your word.
> I have not departed from your laws,
> for you yourself have taught me.
> How sweet are your words to my taste,
> sweeter than honey to my mouth!
> I gain understanding from your precepts;
> therefore I hate every wrong path.
>
> —Psalm 119:101-104

> His divine power has given us everything we need for life and godliness through our knowledge of him who called us by his own glory and goodness. Through these he has given us his very great and precious promises, so that through them you may participate in the divine nature and escape the corruption in the world caused by evil desires.
>
> —2 Peter 1:3, 4

To Study

In our town we have an annual festival called The Taste of Bloomington. Food vendors set up shop all around the town square, and members of the community delight in sampling the best these retailers have to offer. Maybe we need to do some spiritual sampling. In the words of the psalmist, we need to taste and see that God is good.

TASTE AND SEE—GOD'S WORK IS GOOD

As the story of creation and God's ingenious work unfolds, we find a recurring phrase throughout the first chapter of Genesis, "and God saw that it was good." When we meet God for the first time in the Bible he is doing a good work. As a matter of fact, that's the only kind of work he can do! Since God is incapable of anything less, we should be encouraged. The work that he does in our lives, our circumstances, and for our futures can be nothing less than divine goodness.

Wait a minute, you're thinking. *I'm a Christian but I can't say my life has been all good. Where's God's goodness when I'm hurting?* Our pain is not evidence of a lack of God's goodness but proof of a broken world. What God made as *good* in the beginning, our ancestors spiritually trashed shortly thereafter. And there is no such thing as spiritual recycling to bring restoration. Our sins and those of all humanity have tarnished God's creation, and it groans under the weight of our sinful baggage. But God's good work did not end with creation; he reserved his best work for *re-creation*. Through the sacrifice of the ultimate restorer, Jesus, the

TAKE TURNS

1. Talk about some of the good things in your life. How do you know these things are from God?

2. Does anyone have an example of something that seemed bad at the time, but later you discovered the good God was working through that event? Share your experiences.

3. What good works do you want for your family? for your friends? for people you don't even know yet? Can you be a part of making that good happen? How?

work of salvation was completed. Through him we have been re-created, and nothing is sweeter than knowing him as Savior.

Y O U R ↗ S P I N

Take a goodness inventory. Take some time to think about and thank God for these things:

1. List three good things about your working life (whether at home or in a workplace).

2. List three good things about your family life.

3. List three good things about your spiritual life.

If you met a guy today like the apostle Paul, you wouldn't really think of him as a lucky guy. In 2 Corinthians 11:23-29, he tells us this about himself:

I have worked much harder, been in prison more frequently, been flogged more severely, and been exposed to death again and again. Five times I received from the Jews the forty lashes minus one. Three times I was beaten with rods, once I was stoned, three times I was shipwrecked, I spent a night and a day in the open sea, I have been constantly on the move. I have been in danger from rivers, in danger from bandits, in danger from my own countrymen, in danger from Gentiles; in danger in the city, in danger in the country, in danger at sea; and in danger from false brothers. I have labored and toiled and have often gone without sleep; I have known hunger and thirst and have often gone without food; I have been cold and naked. Besides everything else, I face daily the pressure of my concern for all the churches. Who is weak, and I do not feel weak? Who is led into sin, and I do not inwardly burn?

And yet this same guy tells us that "in all things God works for the good of those who love him." Whatever trouble you are facing right now, you can take Paul's word for it. God is working for good—maybe the good of someone more than just you; maybe for your good not today, but somewhere down the road; maybe for a good that is more than you can imagine. We can trust that the same God who created us and sent his Son to die for us wants only good for us.

Did you notice the psalmist's thankfulness for God's Word? "How sweet are your words to my taste, sweeter than honey to my mouth! I gain understanding from your precepts; therefore I hate every wrong path."

Throughout the Bible there is a recurring theme of gratitude for the good words of God; the term *gospel* literally means "good news." You can't really know about God's goodness apart from his Word. The deeper you study, the sweeter it gets.

Just as we mature and grow too old for the CANDY LAND game, adults realize that candy—no matter how sweet—is filled with wasteful (or waist-full) calories and can never satisfy real hunger. Too many of us treat God's Word like candy. We never get past a shallow look at the Bible; we read it as if it is no more meaningful than the imaginary lands on the CANDY LAND game board. This kind of experience can never satisfy the real hunger in our souls—our need to know God.

God calls us to go deeper into his Word with the goal of a more meaningful walk with him. I never cease to be amazed how I always learn something new from Scripture no matter how many times I have read through the same passage. God's Word has the power to change both minds and hearts—it offers satisfying food for the soul.

TAKE TURNS

1. What barriers are there to your Bible study? What would help you study more?

2. Share your favorite Bible story or verses with your small group and explain why that part means so much to you.

3. From your own experience, give your best advice on how to have meaningful Bible study.

Fill in the blanks:

I like doing _____ for others.

I would like to be remembered for being a good _____.

Regarding God's Word, my goal for the future is
_____.

In my desire to honor God I need to change
_____ in my life.

The next time I am tempted I will _____.

TASTE AND SEE—GOD'S WAY IS GOOD

Candy is seductive—have you seen some of those commercials for chocolate treats lately? They tempt, entice, and lure the tastebuds. Why do you think most stores put candy at the checkout counter? Retailers know how hard it is to resist. When I spot a bar of dark chocolate, I don't need any extra prodding to buy it; I need help resisting! For all its momentary joy, unrestrained indulgence to candy can contribute to long-term issues such as dental decay, obesity, and blood sugar problems. Temptation in life works the same way; the momentary joy of giving in to it gives way to devastating, long-term consequences. For that reason, God provides us with a way out—through his direction and guidance for our lives.

Some mistake his wisdom for restriction. God has no desire to destroy our joy; he wants to preserve it. The psalmist had it right: "I have kept my feet from every evil path. . . . I have not departed from your laws. . . . I gain understanding from your precepts; therefore I hate every wrong path." When we understand what God is trying to tell us, we find it easier to choose good paths. Or as Peter penned it, "He has given us his very great and precious promises, so that

> "While forbidden fruit is said to taste sweeter, it usually spoils faster."
>
> —Abigail Van Buren, also known as Dear Abby

CANDY LAND

through them you may participate in the divine nature and escape the corruption in the world caused by evil desires." God's Word helps us escape the corruption of the world.

In the CANDY LAND game, just when the castle is in sight, it is possible to be sent back to some previous position—it might even cost you the game. Trust me—when you yield to temptation, it will set you far back and may even cost you a big win. God's way may not always be the most popular or enviable, but it is the only way to a victorious life. And when you follow his lead, you will know contentment sweeter than candy.

It's Your Move!
How hard is it in our culture to grasp the goodness of God? Many people get blinded by what they believe are apparent contradictions:
- God's goodness versus global human poverty.
- God's goodness versus human devastation from natural catastrophes.
- God's goodness versus human atrocities perpetrated through evil intent.

God's goodness gets overshadowed by the world's evil. Perhaps some people have never seen God at work because they have never witnessed his goodness in us. We need to open their eyes. Words are cheap—good deeds will crack open the door and let some divine light in.

TAKE ⚀ TURNS

1. Where do you turn for help when you are tempted? What has helped you in the past?

2. Has God's Word ever helped you to find a way out of temptation? Did that feel freeing or restraining? Explain.

3. Why do you think temptation exists? Do you know your areas of weakness? How do you use that knowledge to avoid temptation?

As a small group, organize a community action day; mobilize members of your church family to blanket your community with helpful, good deeds. Contact local organizations (schools, Boys and Girls Clubs, Crisis Pregnancy Centers, orphanages, prisons, parks, recreational venues, etc.) and offer your services free of charge. You'll be amazed how your offer to paint, clean, refurbish, weed, mow, rake, restore, build, or tear down will be gratefully received. If you go the extra mile to buy the paint or building supplies, it will make an even greater impact.

Here's another idea for your group. Get permission to use the church property to host helpful events for your neighborhood or community:

- A Bicycle Safety Awareness program where kids are taught about helmets and safety gear, proper safety procedures, rules of the road, and proper bike maintenance.
- A Wellness Fair highlighting local health agencies and their community work.
- A Senior Adult Seminar featuring local professionals on such subjects as Social Security, health issues for the aging, home health care options, and more.

Take an inventory of your community. What unique need isn't being met? If there is something good you can do to meet that need, then DO IT!

BONUS

Extend goodness to others and you will not only sweeten their lives, you will help each other move past the bitterness of a broken world to taste and see that the Lord is good!

POINT

SCRABBLE:
Connecting with Christ's Body

PART ONE—GAME ON

Object of the Game
The SCRABBLE word game requires focus—to win, one must exercise thought, creativity, and a bit of strategy. As you connect your letter tiles with those of your fellow players, take time to reflect on the importance of connecting with others in every day life.

Game Preparation
Like many games, the SCRABBLE board game is designed for four players, so you'll need to have enough boards to fit your group. However, you could play as teams. Alternating players into the game would also make things fun. Have a dictionary on hand to settle word challenges.

> "But if you want a social game—no matter how bad you are, you're always good enough to play. There's mingling, you always play different people, and it's extremely good for thinking."
>
> —Evan Cohen, founder of the Tel-Aviv Scrabble Club

There are some alternatives to the traditional game board. Go to http://www.spintop-games.com/word_game_download/scrabble.html for a free download for your personal computer. Check out the international site at www.scrabble.com for other fun options, including the SCRABBLE game for iPhones and for Facebook.

If you are looking for a decorating theme, try using alphabetic letters of different sizes, shapes, styles, and colors.

*O*ut of work in 1931 due to the Great Depression, architect Alfred Butts developed an idea for a game that used lettered tiles to spell words. He named his prototype game Lexiko, but was unable to secure a patent. By 1938 his ideas had evolved into Criss-Crosswords, but this game garnered little success. In 1947 Alfred Butts was introduced to James Brunot by a mutual friend, and Brunot took over production and marketing of the word game. Still sales lagged until Jack Strauss played it and loved it. As Chairman of New York's famous Macy's Department Store, his opinion carried the day. He put in a large order for the game in 1952, the game caught on nationally, and within two years Brunot's company sold four million games under its new name—SCRABBLE (David Parlett, The Oxford History of Board Games, Oxford: Oxford University Press, 1999, pp. 368-370). And yes, scrabble is a real word that means "to scratch frantically" or "to scribble." (Although Brunot just named the game that because he liked the sound of the word.)

SCRABBLE game tournaments number in the thousands around the world, culminating in the National Scrabble Championship and the World Scrabble Championship (held globally every two years). Interestingly, the largest such tournament in the world is the Thailand International.

Playing by the Rules

For most, playing a SCRABBLE game is challenging enough. But if playing by the rules is too boring for you, here are a few ways to make the game even more interesting:

- Play as two large teams—men versus women, younger versus older, etc.

- Set a time limit of thirty seconds per play (the less time, the more difficult). A stopwatch or timer will be necessary; the clock begins when the previous player has completed his or her word. If the player doesn't start spelling a word before the timer expires, the turn is forfeited.

- Limit the usable words to verbs only or nouns only. Or you can make the game really difficult by using only personal names.

- Limit the number of turns to six. When each person has had the opportunity to spell six words, the game is over and the person with the most points wins.

- Instead of starting with seven tiles and then drawing from the pile as more are needed, start with fifteen tiles. Points don't count. Continue play as long as you can with those fifteen tiles but when you can no longer add to the board, you leave the game. The last person playing is the winner.

Mix things up. You'll be amazed how much fun spelling words can be.

To Eat

There are all kinds of ways you could go with alphabetically themed snacks for your group. Here are just a few ideas:

- What's a SCRABBLE game event without a pot of alphabet soup? Have every person or family bring a can or two of Campbell's Alphabet soup. While the game is heating up, heat the soup so it's ready when you are. I don't know that it qualifies as brain food, but it sure will hit the spot when your brain needs a rest.

- Since vowels are necessary to form English words, serve a healthy "vowel buffet": foods that begin with the letters a, e, i, o, or u. Here are some ideas: apple slices or dried apricots; deviled eggs or elderberry jam on bagel chips; Indian cherries, iceberg lettuce, or low-fat ice cream; oranges or olives; unleavened bread or ugli fruit (OK . . . that one's a stretch, but it really is a tangelo-like citrus fruit grown in Jamaica).

- Or make your own alphabetical trail mix. See recipe below.

MIX IT UP

2 CUPS CANDY-COATED CHOCOLATE MINI CANDIES OR CHOCOLATE CHIPS

2 CUPS RAISINS, DRIED CRANBERRIES, OR OTHER DRIED FRUIT

2 CUPS DRY-ROASTED PEANUTS OR OTHER MIXED NUTS

4 CUPS CEREAL IN THE SHAPE OF ALPHABET LETTERS

Put all the ingredients in a large plastic bag. Secure the bag and toss until all the ingredients are mixed well. Pour into small serving bowls and pass around.

TAKE TURNS

1. What's your favorite word? How does using the right word at the right time connect with others in your daily life?

2. How important do you think it is to study the meaning of the words in the Bible? How much effort do you make to do this?

3. Since the original languages of the Old and New Testaments are Hebrew and Greek respectively, how important, then, is the translation we choose to study? How do words connect us with God?

For Younger Players

There are children's versions of the SCRABBLE game available, but if the children in your group are too young to be good spellers, I would suggest letting them play the CONNECT FOUR game, or a picture domino game, or have them build something together with a connecting blocks or building set. Like the SCRABBLE game, these games can also illustrate the importance of learning how to connect with others.

After the game, talk about how words help us connect with each other. Ask the kids in the group how they would connect with someone who spoke a different language. What could they do to help that person understand and feel connected to everyone else? (If someone in your group speaks a foreign language, have that person role-play with the children to illustrate this point.)

Picking Up the Pieces

Consider three facts about playing the SCRABBLE brand crossword game. First, while winning is the goal in any game, in this crossword game you cannot win alone. Your success depends on the efforts and the words of others.

Second, you cannot arbitrarily spell a word just any old place on the board. You must build on what others have already contributed. It must connect to count.

Finally, to succeed in a SCRABBLE game, one must organize letter tiles and plan ahead. A haphazard player seldom spells the best word or scores the most points.

Consider these three truths in a spiritual context. How do these same lessons apply to community life in the church? What can playing a SCRABBLE game teach us about making connections in God's family?

On the night before the cross, Jesus prayed not only for his disciples but for all of us who would come after them: "My prayer is not for them alone. I pray also for those who will believe in me through their message, that all of them may be one, Father, just as you are in me and I am in you. May they also be in us so that the world may believe that you have sent me" (John 17:20, 21).

What was Jesus' intention when he prayed that prayer, and what can we do twenty centuries later to honor that divine desire? Pray together, asking God to:
- help you see opportunities to connect with others.
- increase your patience with and compassion for others.
- strengthen your commitment to be united in Christ.

SCRABBLE:
Connecting with Christ's Body

PART TWO—POSTGAME BREAKDOWN

Object of the Study

Did you learn any new words after a challenging SCRABBLE game? As you finish this study together, I hope you'll learn some new insights about connecting with others.

Bible Content

Paul offers wise counsel on our togetherness in the family of God. We might call this the SCRABBLE passage because it instructs us about the importance of connectedness within the body of Christ.

> For by the grace given me I say to every one of you: Do not think of yourself more highly than you ought, but rather think of yourself with sober judgment, in accordance with the measure of faith God has given you. Just as each of us has one body with many members, and these members do not all have the same function, so in Christ we who are many form one body, and each member belongs to all the others. We have different gifts, according to the grace given us. If a man's gift is prophesying, let him use it in proportion to his faith. If it is serving, let him serve; if it is teaching, let him teach; if it is encouraging, let him encourage; if it is contributing to the needs of others, let him give generously; if it is leadership, let him govern diligently; if it is showing mercy, let him do it cheerfully.
>
> —Romans 12:3-8

To Study

You won't gain many points in the SCRABBLE game or in life if you constantly play *I* by itself. That this personal pronoun stands alone as a one-letter word is significant; when you're stuck on I, you usually end up all alone.

Did you notice Paul's first warning? "Do not think of yourself more highly than you ought." My friend Jeff Faull offers this as one of his favorite quotes: "The smallest package in the world is the person who is wrapped up in himself." Think that's an exaggeration? A license branch in Illinois had so many applications for the personalized license plate "#1" that the branch manager put it on his own vehicle rather than decide who else should have it. In our me-first culture it's tough to maintain a balanced perspective, but in God's kingdom it's impossible to have a relationship with him while being self-consumed!

TAKE TURNS

1. What do you feel when you find yourself in the company of a self-focused person? How do you react when he talks only of himself?

2. Have you ever been self-consumed? If so, did it negatively affect your relationships? What made you realize you were being self-centered?

3. Paul says to think of ourselves with "sober judgment." What would that look like for you?

ONE BODY—MANY PARTS

I heard a story about an elderly lady who decided to travel the globe and applied for her passport. The government clerk said, "You must first take a loyalty oath; raise your right hand, please." She did. The clerk continued. "Do you swear to defend the Constitution of the United States against all its enemies, domestic or foreign?" The ady's face paled, she slowly lowered her hand, and with trembling voice asked, "Do have to do that all by myself?"

TAKE TURNS

1. When the organs of your body stop working together, you get sick. What are some signs when the body of Christ is sick?

2. Which should be our priority and why: church growth or church health?

3. How well does your church do at making its members feel a part of one body? How do you think this could be improved?

None of us want to face the challenges and stresses of life all alone. That's a rimary reason why God created the church and called it the body of Christ. God new it would be nearly impossible to grow our faith if we had to live life alone. God esigned the church to sustain, encourage, strengthen, and hold us accountable ntil we die. Without the church we won't survive spiritually. Have you ever heard omeone say, "I'm a Christian but I don't want to belong to any church?" That's like aying, "I'm a point guard, but I don't want to be a part of a basketball team." It just oesn't make sense.

We have been made in the image of a relational, triune God—God the Father, iod the Son, and God the Holy Spirit. Just look at how God has illustrated relational onnectedness in his creation around us. The universe isn't just a random display f heavenly bodies, it is connected and orderly. Your physical body is another exam- le of harmonious relationships. Each day the heart beats 100,000 times, faithfully umping our blood through 60,000 miles of blood vessels (if laid end to end). Your ody supports 45 miles of nerves in the skin. Nerve impulses to and from the brain ravel at 170 miles per hour (except during sermons when they slow to nocturnal speeds). Every part of your body works together harmoniously for the good of the whole. Our best spiritual value is not found in our individuality but in our connect edness to one another. To have a healthy spiritual body we have to work togethe harmoniously in the church to be who God created us to be—*his* body.

YOUR SPIN

1. Do you feel like you should take an active part in including others in the church, or do you feel like this is the respon- sibility of the church staff? How does reading Paul's words, "each member belongs to all the others," affect your think- ing about this subject?

2. Do you feel like your church is your family, that you are part of one body? Why or why not? How much of that feeling depends on your own actions and how much depends on the actions of others?

3. Think about the roles you play in your church. What more could you do to reach out to others as part of the body of Christ?

MANY PARTS—ONE PURPOSE

Consider these principles from God's Word, also illustrated by your SCRABBLE game experience:

- Accept who you are. The challenge in the SCRABBLE game is winning with the letters pulled from the pile. We can't choose the letters we want we play with the luck of the draw. That's life. We can't choose our DNA the challenge is winning with the way we are wired. Don't waste you limited time and energy wishing you were someone else. Be grateful fo who God created you to be.

- Work with what you have. In the game we want the high-point-value letters like *Z* and *Q*, but they are virtually worthless unless you have one-point vowel to put with them. Undoubtedly, you will know someon more gifted than you, but in the body of Christ, every part is vital. We work and serve together as a team, not as individuals. Nothing is ever accomplished until those with ordinary gifts connect with those who have unique gifts to honor the Lord.

- You may be thinking, *In the great SCRABBLE game of life, I'm the blank tile—nothing, nada, zero, the big goose egg—I'm worthless!* Hold on, nothing could be further from the truth. Remember, the blank tile in this letter game is the most versatile piece in the whole game. If you haven't discovered your talents yet, don't worry. You're the piece that fits any and everywhere!

Make a difference where you live. Medical science reveals that the body replaces the skin cells at such a rate that every seven years, you have all new skin. What would happen if your body stopped replacing the cells? Your outer shell would be a decaying mess, right? So it is with the body of Christ— it needs new cells too. It's not enough to connect and build relationships with people inside the church family; God has also gifted you to connect with people outside the family. If we don't do this, the body of Christ will grow ill, shrivel up, and die.

"We are incredibly, incurably relational. God has designed the need for community into the spiritual DNA of every person."

—Rick Atchley, minister, Richland Hills Church of Christ

TAKE TURNS

1. Look at Romans 12:6-8 again. Which of the listed gifts seems more valuable to you?

2. In your opinion which gift most benefits the church?

3. Why do you suppose Paul draws no distinction between the gifts? How is one who encourages as valuable as one who teaches? How do we use our gifts "in proportion to our faith"?

Back in 1994, country singer Tracy Lawrence recorded the song "If the World Had a Front Porch." The lyrics remind us how society was more neighborly in the past, and that the front porch was the place where we connected with others. believe God wants his church to become a front porch to a broken world:

- a place where people can relax from the stress of life.

- a place where people feel welcomed by the family.

- a place where the lost can connect with the Father again.

YOUR SPIN

The following statements are either true or false in your life. Use this privately or as a group to assess your relational attitudes.

1._____ When I am discouraged I turn to others at church for encouragement.

2._____ A friend at church gets the promotion I wanted; I am genuinely happy for him.

3._____ I made some poor choices and now I'm suffering the consequences. I hope the church doesn't find out about my mistakes.

4._____ When others at church are dealing with tough times, I make myself readily available to help without expecting anything in return.

5._____ I like to give generously to fellow Christians who are struggling, without their knowing who sent the gift.

What are some steps you can take to develop godly attitudes toward others?

t's Your Move!

s a small group consider some projects to help others connect in the church amily:

- Host a dessert buffet at the church building and invite folks who are new to the church to come and connect with one another.

- Help start another small group to connect people who are not involved in the body life of the church. Include the new folks in your group for a few sessions (to learn how a healthy small group interacts), then spin them off on their own.

- Do you know any senior adults in your church who are alone? Invite them to visit your small group and have them talk about what life was like when they were young, how they raised their families, and what they accomplished in their careers. Use that as a stepping stone to build a new friendship with someone who still needs a connection in the body of Christ but may feel forgotten.

Get creative—think of other ways you can be more relational in your church amily.

If God spared no expense in bridging the relational divide to connect with us, then we have no excuse for being less than relational in his family. Get connected. God made it a priority—we should too.

ABOUT THE AUTHOR

Tom Ellsworth has served as the preaching minister at Sherwood Oaks Christia
Church in Bloomington, Indiana, since 1981. It was there that he delivered th
sermon series that became the seed of inspiration for this book. Tom is gratefu
for the friendship, spiritual insight, and encouraging leadership of his peers i
ministry Jeff Faull, Gary Johnson, Sean Olson, and Billy Strother, who all worke
together with him to develop "The Games People Play" sermon series.

In his free time, he enjoys aviation history and tinkering with his 1948 Chrysle
Mostly he loves spending time with his wife, Elsie, and their two grown daughters
together with their families. Tom is also the author of the Standard Publishin
resources *It's Your Move—Out Loud* and *Beyond Your Backyard* (with *Beyond You
Backyard Group Member Discussion Guide*), and co-authored *Preaching Jame
* (Chalice Press).